THE SAILING LOVE

Maintaining A Love Connection In Today's Self-Centered Culture

MARCUS PALMER

The Sailing Love

Maintaining A Love Connection In Today's Self-Centered Culture

ISBN: 979-8-3664823-7-0

Table of Contents

INTRODUCTION

Maintaining a love connection in today's self-centered culture is difficult. Breakups frequently occur for no apparent cause but for reasons that might have been overcome if only there had been the will to do so. If there's one thing I've learned in the last decade of being in a committed relationship, it's that love isn't a sensation. Love is a decision. Each day, we are faced with several opportunities to demonstrate our love to those we care about. It is entirely up to us whether we do it or not. Sometimes the little things keep a couple together for a long period. Unfortunately, the majority of individuals overlook the indications or, worse, quit looking.

So, you're in a relationship and looking for strategies to strengthen your bond and endure longer? Understanding how to make a relationship last depends heavily on the circumstances of your current connection. There should be nothing to worry about if you are currently in a position where you demonstrate tremendous comfort and straightforward responsibilities. Not everyone wants to take things for granted when it comes to relationships. As a result, more work and greater understanding are necessary to ensure that your connection bond becomes stronger by the day.

Beholding the person you love close to your body and heart, connecting psychologically, emotionally, and physically, is one of the nicest experiences in the world. We may not know it, but our close connections teach us a great deal about the people we care about, as well as about ourselves.

Being connected is a profound emotional bond characterized by friendship and affection. It might be platonic or sexual in nature. Regardless of what the quality of your relationship is, it is inevitable to have disagreements with your spouse since you spend so much time together and have different personalities, tastes, and needs. When partners disagree, it is an indication that the relationship needs to mature. If you feel estranged from your partner, you must develop new methods to interact and connect with them. It is a chance to develop new abilities while being intimate with your spouse. The cornerstone of love is intimacy, and the road to achieving it is a voyage of personal growth.

If you're seeking perfection, look within yourself rather than outside of your spouse. Everything else will fall in place if you do your bit to be the greatest partner you can be.

Love is all seeing and all accepting, which implies you accept all of your partner's shortcomings. Your relationship can only thrive if you accept responsibility for the issues rather than merely passing blame. Accountability generates responsibility, which fosters clear, clean, and balanced communication with ourselves and others.

To appreciate the significance of love and intimacy in a relationship, you must first understand that without love and affection, we are unable to pursue self-actualization, which is the desire to realize our societal potential. Happiness in any relationship comes from being and aspiring to be the right partner, not from finding the perfect spouse.

CHAPTER ONE

COMMUNICATION

I'm sure you've heard the expression, "communication is the key to every relationship." It may seem corny, but it's true. I believe it is quite easy to convince people that communication is essential in a successful relationship, but it is much more difficult to explain how to communicate. We'll never be able to unlock the door to good communication if we're never taught how to utilize this key.

Communication may be described as a variety of things, but my favorite is "the successful conveying or exchanging of ideas and sentiments." I usually say I'm a great talker, but in order to be a great communicator, I also have to be a great listener. Communication is expressing oneself in a healthy manner, listening to your partner when they do the same, and truly hearing and digesting what the other person has to say.

Effective communication is a crucial component of every good partnership and is an important component of all partnerships. Of course, every relationship has ups and downs, but a good communication style may help you cope with disagreement and establish a stronger, healthier partnership.

We frequently hear how vital communication is, but not what it is or how we can use it in our relationships. Communication is essential in relationships if you want to have a happy, healthy relationship. It's also not about making small conversation. It's fine to ask your spouse how their day went, but if you want an outstanding connection, you must go further. Understanding how communication works in a relationship is all about meeting your partner's needs. To increase communication in your relationship, learn to listen first, then discuss.

Clear communication in a relationship

Communicate with each other. You can't read your partner's mind, no matter how well you know and love each other. We must speak clearly to avoid misconceptions that might lead to pain, anger, resentment, or bewilderment. A relationship requires two individuals, and each person has various communication methods and requirements. Couples must ensure they develop a communication style that works for them. Healthy communication styles need practice and dedication. Communication is never going to be great all of the time. When speaking with your spouse, be straightforward, so your message is heard and comprehended. Check that you comprehend what your spouse is saying.

When communicating with your spouse, aim to:

- Make time to communicate without being interrupted by other people or distractions such as phones, laptops, or television.
- Consider what you want to say.
- Make what you want to say clear.
- Make your message clear so that your spouse hears it correctly and knows what you mean.
- Discuss what is going on and how it impacts you.
- Use 'I' expressions such as 'I need,' 'I desire,' and 'I feel' to express what you want, need, and feel.

- Accept responsibility for your emotions.
- Pay attention to your spouse. For the time being, set aside your own ideas and attempt to grasp their goals, feelings, needs, and desires (this is called empathy).
- Share your good sentiments with your spouse, such as what you like and admire about them, as well as how important they are to you.
- Be mindful of your tone of speech.
- Negotiate and realize that you don't always have to be right. If the topic isn't that essential to you, try to let it go or agree to disagree.

We may express a lot without saying it when we communicate. Our body posture, tone of voice, and facial expressions all send a message. These nonverbal communication methods might convey how we feel about them to the other person.

If our words do not match our sentiments, it is typically nonverbal communication that is 'heard' and trusted. Saying 'I love you' to your lover in a flat, bored tone of voice, for example, sends two very different meanings. Examine whether your body language matches what you're saying.

Pose open-ended inquiries

Communication is more than just telling each other about your days and what you had for lunch. It's about going deep and getting to know this individual as thoroughly as possible. Of course, it's not always simple to go deep, especially for people who have never felt comfortable discussing their emotions. And it's not necessary to have a heart-to-heart with everyone.

There are methods to accomplish this without putting your significant other under duress. In place of asking 'yes' or 'no' questions such as "Did you have a nice day?" Ask more open-ended queries, such as "How was your day?" Yes, they may react with a quick non-answer ("good," "fine," or "the same"), but asking open-ended questions allows them to share more if they like. Keep in mind that not everyone is easily opened up to. Be tolerant of your spouse if they do not always share. We create limits around our emotions, and each person's borders are unique. So, be aware of and respectful of their emotional limits, just as they should be aware of and respectful of yours.

Finally, the better you get to know your significant other, the more open and honest you may be with one other. And honesty begets trust, which are two crucial elements of a good relationship.

Try not to read their minds

You can sometimes tell how someone is feeling just by glancing at them. Unfortunately, it's not always simple, and let's face it: no matter how much we want to be mind readers, we aren't and shouldn't have to be. So, if you're unsure how your spouse feels, ask them.

If you're the one who's keeping things to yourself and expecting your spouse to read your mind, appreciate the fact that your partner is making an effort by asking you what's up rather than ignoring the situation. When you're ready to talk about it, do your best to let them know how you're feeling. It's unhealthy to claim you're fine when you're not and then blame your spouse for not noticing. To the best of your abilities, be honest about how you feel and attempt to communicate it in a healthy way before it blows up and someone says something they regret. Being straightforward is always preferable to being passive-aggressive.

If your spouse is the one who is being passive-aggressive, try telling them that it isn't good for either of you when they aren't honest about how they feel. Of course, it's wonderful when we know each other so well that we can virtually read each other's minds and know precisely what to say at the perfect times, but we're all human, and we may make errors or miss signs that are clear to our partner or vice versa. It's critical that you both make an effort to understand each other better while also being patient with one another.

Conversations are bidirectional

Take note of how many times you say "I," "You," or "We" when communicating with your spouse. If the talk is largely about you, it isn't a conversation. Remember to return the focus to your significant other and inquire about their feelings, thoughts, and what is going on with them. What is the context if you find yourself saying "You" a lot? Are you blaming and pointing fingers?

Relationships are about both individuals, and both should have an equal say in the decisions that are made. Both parties must feel heard and free to express themselves. It's crucial to let your spouse know if you feel that he or she is dominating the discussion and you can't get a word in. They may be unaware that they are monopolizing the discourse. Conversations are like a tennis match; they should flow effortlessly from one person to the next.

Schedule Talking Time

Myself and my partner recently moved in together, and almost everyone told us that it's a "make or break" scenario for couples. We were both anxious, but we had the cocky attitude of 'we got this.' We've always been terrific at speaking with each other openly and honestly. We had no clue how living together would alter how we communicated, but it did.

We fought continuously during the first three weeks we were together. We were so irritated by the squabbling (rather than the issue at hand) that we ended up bickering over the fact that we were bickering. Do you have headache yet? Yes, we had one for approximately three weeks. But, we ultimately sat down and spoke it out because we were not in that relationship.

Because we were now sharing the same place, we had to learn an entirely new way of being with one another. We discussed what was important (such as how to spend our money) and what was ultimately unimportant (who takes out the trash). Talking about those things was critical because we would never have understood what was important to the other person if we hadn't sat down to talk about it.

We eventually realized that none of our squabbles were about the issues we were arguing over but rather about not feeling heard or valued. We decided to start what we call "Bae Sesh," a weekly "session" when we set aside an hour to express ourselves in a judgment-free environment. This gives us a sense of being heard and valued.

Obviously, our hour-long "Bae Sesh" isn't for everyone, but it works for us. Because of weekly Bae Sessions, we've been able to prevent greater disputes, actively listen to each other, bond, and feel closer to each other. Of course, we communicate every day, but with both of us so busy with work and life, it's good to make time for something a bit deeper.

Recognize Nonverbal Cues

If your spouse answers, "My day was okay," but their tone sounds frustrated, disturbed, or furious, there may be something more going on that they aren't ready to express. Communication is about more than simply the words we use; it is also about how we use them. Our tone and attitude reveal far more than the words that come out of our mouths. It truly is a talent to be able to pick up on nonverbal signs. Examine your significant other's facial expressions, hands (are they trembling/fidgety?), and body language (Are they making eye contact? Are their arms crossed?), and pay attention to their tone of voice.

When communication in a relationship develops but our expectations do not, there is dissonance, and we must check in with ourselves and our partner to fix it. But first, here's a basic rule of thumb for how communication tends to ebb and flow over a relationship. Continue reading and attempt to predict where you could end up.

Tell them what you require of them

Sometimes I simply want to rant and be validated by my spouse, responding, "Yeah, that truly stinks; I'm sorry!" Sometimes I need advice. As I previously stated, none of us are mind readers; therefore, it's critical to keep your spouse informed so that you're both on the same page. "I need to scream right now, and I'm not asking for any advice, just your support," or "I truly need your input on this matter," I will let them know exactly what you need at that time.

Being straightforward about what you want might also help to reduce miscommunication or tension in a particular circumstance. We may avoid avoidable arguments caused by a misinterpretation by informing them ahead of time.

* * *

Communication is a talent; there is always a potential for development. Work with your spouse to figure out how to keep good communication going and stay on the same page. Be as straightforward, direct, courteous, and considerate as possible, whether through a Bae Sesh or simply making a concerted effort to open out to one another.

Be present in your relationship in order to increase communication and grasp what your spouse is saying genuinely. Create some time and devote yourself entirely to conversing with your partner. They must sincerely believe they have your undivided attention and are your top priority.

When you're angry and upset or working on activities that take you away from your relationship, listening and being truly present, attentive, and thoughtful is tough. This is a natural aspect of life, but it should not be used as an excuse to avoid communicating in relationships. Remember that closeness, love, and trust are formed when things are difficult, not when times are easy. We would never advance or evolve if we quit at the first hint of opposition. Take advantage of these opportunities to learn how to cope with conflict and stress in a healthy way, and watch as you and your spouse develop and bloom.

CHAPTER TWO

"PLEASE" AND "THANK YOU" SHOULD BE USED

When I was younger, my mother always told me to address adults as "Sir" and "Ma'am" and to always say "please" and "thank you." If it took her a lifetime, she was going to pound manners into me. Sure, having to go through the drill every time I went to a friend's house was annoying, but I am grateful that she instilled those words in my vocabulary.

Though we don't like being addressed as "Sir" and "Ma'am" when we're young, there's something special about the respect that comes with the title. When I address someone as "Sir" or "Ma'am," it means that I respect them.

Our parents instilled in us the value of being courteous. We are told that saying "please" and "thank you" is essential for expressing respect and appreciation. But how far should we go with this? Is it necessary to be so polite to our intimate partner? Is there intimacy and assumption of trust that eliminates the need for such polite displays?

We'd all probably agree that developing trust in any relationship, especially an intimate one, necessitates a high level of respect, kindness, and sensitivity. When we become numb to how we affect each other or take each other for granted, our relationships spiral downward. But how important is it to say "thank you" politely whenever our partner does something nice for us? Is it our responsibility to thank our partners every time they pass the salt or hold the door open for us?

This is a very complicated issue; a careless, cavalier attitude would be: "You know I appreciate you, why do I need to thank you?" People, in my experience, feel more connected when there is a steady flow of gratitude toward one another. Relationships require nurturing in order to thrive.

However, such expressions of gratitude are most effective when they are genuine, spontaneous, and heartfelt. If saying "please" and "thank you" becomes rote behavior or an obligation, the purpose of using these words is defeated to foster connection and love while maintaining an atmosphere of goodwill and respect. When we feel obligated or under pressure to be polite, intimacy suffers.

"Please" and "thank you" are also respectful messages. "Please" softens the blow of a request. When a small child approaches and says, "Make me a snack!" we wonder, "And who do you think you are, Squirt?". We are much more open to the request if that same child walks up and says, "May I have a snack, please?" We want to give to those who don't take us for granted, don't expect anything in return, and value what we do. Maybe Mom didn't want the rest of the world to groan when they saw me approaching.

People's requirements differ. Some people feel more connected when they hear "please" and "thank you" in their everyday conversation. Others may regard such displays of politeness as an unnecessary or even irritating convention. Words are cheap to them — or at least not as useful as actions that demonstrate love. Respect and kindness are more meaningful to them when they are embodied nonverbally in one's demeanor, tone of voice, and sensitivity to their feelings and needs.

Those who take the time to say "thank you" acknowledge that someone else went out of their way to improve their lives. "I do not take you for granted," they say. You are a gift to me. What you did was significant in my life. You are greatly appreciated." Some relationships are genuinely lacking in appreciation. If you want to water and nourish your sweetie, start by showing even the smallest amount of respect. Say "please" when you want something. Say "thank you" when your sweetie does something nice for you, even if it is something you take for granted.

Providing Verbal Appreciation

There are numerous things for which we can express gratitude if we pay attention. We can offer a "thank you" or "I appreciate that" when we genuinely feel grateful for words or actions that touch us in some way when it feels "right" and natural. Here are some examples of things our partner might do for us for which we should be grateful:

- Calls us at work to see how we're doing when they know we're struggling with something.
- Goes out in the rain to take out the garbage.
- It's a fantastic meal for us.
- Shares something they like about us.

- Pays close attention to what we want to say.
- Goes out of their way to please us, such as watching a movie they didn't like or visiting our family.

Hearing such gratitude fosters trust and connection. It indicates that our partner notices what we do for them rather than taking us for granted.

Nonverbal Expression of Appreciation

Verbal appreciation promotes connection, but nonverbal displays of appreciation should not be overlooked. A smile on our partner's face may move us more than traditional words of gratitude. A knowing look or a smile can say more than words ever could. As our partner serves a delicious casserole, we may smile or make pleasure sounds to express our delight and gratitude. Alternatively, a heartfelt comment with an inflection that conveys praise and appreciation, such as "Wow! you're amazing," may delight our partner more than a tame "thank you" that lacks feeling.

As an experiment, pay attention when you feel grateful for something your partner or a friend does for you. Can you come up with some words to express that? Is it possible to express gratitude in nonverbal ways, such as through your tone of voice, facial expression, or eye contact?

It's especially important to show our partners and friends that we appreciate them and don't take them for granted during difficult times like the coronavirus.

You might feel awkward at first if you're not used to heartfelt expressions of gratitude. You might find it very satisfying gradually.

When you express gratitude, it tends to come back to you. Giving what you want is not always easy, but it is a wise way to get more of what you want.

Getting Natural

If saying please and thank you does not come naturally to you, I would still encourage you to try. You can begin by thanking your sweetie in the least awkward way possible, working your way up to heartfelt, eye-to-eye thanks.

We all want our efforts to be noticed and rewarded. Showering your spouse with gratitude (to varying degrees depending on his or her personality) is equivalent to watering his or her soul.

People who are thankful have lighter hearts, less anxiety, and more hope. So, expressing gratitude will not only benefit your spouse and your relationship, but it will also benefit you!

There are numerous ways to express your appreciation. And, if you truly understand why you chose your partner (or why you chose to stay together), expressing your gratitude should be simple.

What could be more nurturing of a happy relationship than expressing how much you appreciate and care for each other?

By incorporating it into your relationship on a daily basis, it will become second nature to you.

CHAPTER THREE

MAKE TIME FOR DATE NIGHTS

They call it the seven-year itch because falling in love isn't all that difficult. Are you still in love? That's a completely different story. Those first butterflies can help you feel like you're the luckiest person alive. However, as time passes, we become acquainted with our partners' habits and reactions. They start to become predictable, and predictable can also mean boring. Of course, this does not mean that every love affair is doomed, but the spark in many relationships fades. We've all seen it happen: people grow apart. One issue is that the quirks you find endearing at the beginning of a relationship can become irritating or even annoying over time. It's possible that the predictability factor is to blame: when love is new, everything becomes more vivid and exciting. The vibrancy then appears to fade. Here comes the antidote: the solution to the ravages of time. Make date night part of the spice that keeps things exciting if you want to retain the excitement of new love for an extended period of time—possibly even forever.

Date night is often one of the first things to go as life's responsibilities pile up. We believe that we are "close enough" to our partners or that having a date night is considered a luxury rather than an essential part of a happy and healthy relationship. Even if we want to go on a date night, who has the time? We're exhausted after a long day, and all we want to do is lie down and relax.

This is a very dangerous slope that most couples do not anticipate. Yes, it is difficult, but date night is essential for maintaining a healthy relationship. Particularly with the added stress of daily life. Date night helps us communicate better, feel closer, learn more about our partner (yes, even after years of being together), raise

happier children, and extend the life of our relationships.

Date Night Keeps the Relationship Sparkling

I understand your skepticism. You've heard that getting off the daily grind of life and recapturing the ambiance of earlier days can help restore romance or intimacy. But who has time for that? Our jobs require us to work on different schedules; wouldn't it take more energy to connect our schedules? After all, isn't it natural for the first flush of love to fade? I understand. However, the time to attend to the relationship is not when it is fading but when love is still in bloom. Date night can relieve

stress rather than add to it, and it could lead to a lifetime of happiness.

According to studies, shared activities help maintain relationships; however, both now and in the future, positive, stress-free activities and relationship quality necessitate both of you wanting thc activity and the outcome it may bring. According to studies, the quality of the connection should be prioritized before there is a threat to it. The majority of people who enjoyed their date night activities said it improved their relationship even after the event; they felt they had learned more about their partner and could apply higher levels of relationship skills.

Date Night Goes Above and Beyond

Everyday maintenance is important, but date night can add that extra something. It provides opportunities to openly discuss thoughts and feelings, maintain a cheerful and affectionate demeanor, and provide assurances associated with commitment and satisfaction to the partner; it also predicts whether the relationship will last for 8 weeks. According to research, date nights have positive effects such as increased commitment, concern for the partner, more time to understand the significant other, shared fun time, and improved communication. If these characteristics are willingly exhibited by both couple members, they are unquestionably long-term relationship material.

Date Concepts

So, what activities are most effective in keeping a relationship healthy and thriving? According to research, novel, exciting, and arousing activities increase closeness more than routine ones. According to a source, activities that are "adventurous, passionate, sexual, playful, romantic, spontaneous, and requiring a high level of alertness and involvement" are the ones that best reinforce closeness and commitment. According to one study, partners who shared skydiving had higher levels of relationship satisfaction than those who did not.

I suppose you're invested in the relationship if you're willing to jump out of a plane for your partner! However, closeness was reported to be highest when activities included a balance of safety and risk: no one wanted to explain to the ER doctor that they were engaging in risky behavior to keep their relationship healthy. A vacation or a day at the beach ranks first in terms of fostering closeness and intimacy. Shopping, gardening, and setting aside a designated time for intimacy are all activities that work best. Being aware of your partner's preferences for any of these activities could be the spark that keeps the fires burning. Communication and honesty are essential in any activity and any successful relationship;

accommodating the partner was a critical aspect of both parties' positive relationship evaluation. Finally, choose activities that do not cause anxiety; studies show that stress-free events promote closer relationships and are associated with higher relationship quality. Show that you're invested in avoiding stress! Don't sign up for an activity you don't enjoy just to make date night work. That shared mutually appealing activity exists: go find it.

The Importance of Quality Time

More important than the activity itself, however, is the willingness of both parties to invest in spending time together. According to research, positive activity outcomes are determined less by what couples do and more by how they feel about doing them together. Activities are chosen for their ability to increase closeness and perform better than activities chosen for their "fun factor." Furthermore, lower closeness is reported when one-half of the couple believes the partner is only half-heartedly enthusiastic about the activity. According to one study, men who were not eager to participate in shared activities with their partners were among the couples who did not reach the three-month mark of the study.

Arguably the most common deterrent to date night is time. We come home from work exhausted, only to have to catch up with chores, kids, pets, family, etc. It's exhausting. It feels like by the time we finish, it's already time to go to sleep and repeat the cycle the next day. How do we make time for date night like this?

Luckily, you can do many simple, quick things to make time for date night. You don't need a lot of time. Just schedule 1 single hour every month. Yes, really, just 1 hour a month is all it takes. You don't have to get fancy and make reservations at a fancy restaurant an hour away. You don't have to pack up for an entire weekend away. Just set aside 1 hour where it's just you and your partner together, alone. Set the kids up with their favorite show, movie, or game, and use that time for your date night.

Couples who incorporate date nights into their lives report improved communication, increased affection and gratitude for one another, and a desire to spend more time together. Date night provides welcome entertainment, allowing couples to refocus on critical issues without distractions. The date night experience shows that the partners value their relationship and are willing to invest in it. During enjoyable events, both contribute to relieving stress for the other. One of the additional significant benefits? Date night leads to more shared time, which increases sexual satisfaction.

What's The Message?

If you have a good thing going and want your relationship to last, don't wait for signs of trouble. Spice up your life now and reap the long-term benefits. Perhaps tonight, while sitting on the sofa, put a mischievous gleam in your eye, tilt your head to the side, and put it out there: "Hey honey, how about a date tonight?"

CHAPTER FOUR

ACKNOWLEDGE EACH OTHER'S STRENGTHS AND WEAKNESSES

Many couples end up divorcing because they fail to recognize each other's strengths and weaknesses. They either feel like they're competing with each other, or one of them is weaker and will soon become a burden. Relationships do not work like that. They are formed out of love, trust, friendship, and respect, not out of convenience.

When you're in a relationship, you should have the courage to accept your partner's flaws and work your way up from there (and vice versa). This allows you to inspire each other to become better partners and individuals, allowing your relationship to grow.

Understanding a partner's strengths or weaknesses may be easier than understanding their weaknesses. Because weakness is frequently not present as it is, it is sometimes obscured by unrealistic expectations. Recognizing a partner's weaknesses and strengths is essential in developing a healthy relationship. In a romantic relationship, you and your partner should discover what each other is good at. It is also necessary to comprehend the flaws. Wouldn't it be more fun if you had a partner who knows exactly who you are? The goal is to comprehend so that the relationship can flourish. However, we have a tendency to judge a partner objectively rather than objectively.

Recognizing the strengths and weaknesses of each individual who has made a long-term commitment will make it easier to find creative solutions. This inventive solution concerns partners and their social relationships. For example, how to keep a partner's secret and trust and be trusted to keep it. Mutual trustworthiness and the ability to keep secrets close must be founded on understanding each other's strengths and weaknesses. Recognizing and accepting partners as they are can help to support mental health conditions mutually. Anxiety is a problem that frequently manifests itself in relationships. Accommodating a partner's anxieties as part of trusting a relationship is always available to each other. As a result, you and your partner can rely on each other to be more 'human.'

Weakness is a person's most vulnerable aspect. Everyone has this side, albeit with different motivators. However, in most cases, we don't require much active assistance to feel supported. Even the smallest gestures can convey support. Knowing what your partner has in common, such as their vulnerabilities, weaknesses, strengths, needs, and how to support one another, is an important aspect for each partner. That is, the criteria for a partner who is tall, handsome, and shares a hobby may be insufficient. Subtle factors such as knowing, accepting, and supporting each other in specific ways are common in mature and successful relationships.

Identifying Your Strengths

This always amazes us, but in our experience, couples frequently do not have a clear picture of their relationship's strengths. What is the reason for this? We live in a problem-solving culture: Almost always, the emphasis is on defining problems and finding solutions. As a result, couples frequently have a clear picture of what's wrong with their relationship but haven't spent any time focusing on their strengths. The issue with this approach is that rely on our strengths to solve our problems. And, without an understanding of our own strengths, it is difficult to see how problems can be solved successfully. The emphasis here will be on the strengths of your relationship with your partner and how these strengths can be used to further strengthen your bond. Filling out the American Couple Strengths Inventory is a good way to start a conversation about a couple's strengths. Many couples are surprised to learn about their own strengths. "I'm always thinking about our problems, but this is the first time I've really thought about our strengths," a spouse may say.

It's amazing how many good things we have in our marriage."

A useful model for describing the strengths of couples and families. we believe, includes six major strengths: commitment to the couple and the family; appreciation and affection for each other; positive communication; a sense of spiritual well-being and shared values; enjoyable time together; and the ability to effectively manage stress and crises. Each quality builds on another, and if a couple has one, they are very likely to have many more. Keep in mind that you will find strength if you look for it in your relationship, and if these strengths are nurtured, they will grow. Fill out the couple strengths inventory together to start this fascinating process.

Talking About Your Strengths

It's important to remember that each partner will likely have a different perspective on their relationship and what's going on in the family. Even if you eat at the same table and witness the same events in your and your extended family's lives, you are very likely to see things differently. "We don't see things the way they are," say professionals who work with families. We see the world as we are." In other words, each person sees the world through her or his own set of perception lenses. For example, what appears to be a friendly joke to one person may appear to another to be a very hostile attack. Or, what appears to one person as a generous offer of assistance may appear to another as an imposition. Couples re very likely to interpret what is going on in their relationship and in their family in very different ways. This is why it is critical to constantly discuss and compare your perceptions of what is going on with your partner. You may be very pleased with what is happening, but your partner may be very upset. Only open and honest communication will smooth your path together. Loved ones don't always agree, and it would be foolish to try to eliminate all disagreements. Rather, recognize that you will naturally have different points of view and then enjoy developing new strategies to ensure that your different perspectives on the world mean you can still live happily together. Discuss your different perceptions of your couple's strengths and then reach an agreement on the strengths on which you can both agree and the areas of potential growth on which you can both agree.

* * *

Understand that the difference between people who are successful despite their weaknesses and people who struggle because of their weaknesses is in their perspective and approach to their shortcomings.

Create your own personal affirmations to help you feel good about yourself. You are creating your own personal affirmations, and positive truths about yourself, by identifying your strengths and weaknesses and writing down how, why, and when you possess each one. Make the most of your strengths. Consider something you want to be more confident about doing.

www.ingramcontent.com/pod-product-compliance
Lightning Source LLC
LaVergne TN
LVHW090133160826
845673LV00017B/2458

* 9 7 9 8 3 6 6 4 8 2 3 7 0 *